my emotions A JOURNAL FOR TEENS

my emotions

A JOURNAL FOR TEENS

Guided Exercises to Help You Express, Understand, and Manage Emotions

Joy A. Hartman, MSW, LCSW

ROCKRIDGE PRESS

This book is dedicated to B who
likes to tell me she has NO feelings,
to E who has ALL the feelings
and to W who navigates them both with ease.

THIS JOURNAL BELONGS TO:

....

contents

Managing Your Feelings

Being a teenager is a wild ride. I like to say that figuring out your emotions during the teen years is like driving the world's most powerful race car. Your feelings have a lot of power; they're fast, exhilarating, and come out of nowhere. Your emotions can take you on a wild ride, and sometimes may even crash and burn.

Keeping a super-powerful race car on the track takes practice and skills. The same goes for managing your emotions. However, most teenagers are still learning the skills to correctly steer the emotional power they're experiencing.

Your emotions are the window to who you are. They impact your beliefs about yourself and how you interact with the world. Yet there isn't anything about your emotions that is predictable, especially during the teen years. It takes training to truly understand what you're feeling when life doesn't go as perfectly as you planned—which, speaking from experience, happens more often than not.

This journal can help.

Before I get into the details of this journal, let me introduce myself. My name is Joy Hartman and I am a mental health therapist who specializes in working with teenagers. For past 30 years I've counseled teens in their homes, in foster care, in residential treatment, in group homes, in schools, and in the community. Even though my clients come from different backgrounds, the one thing that is common among all teenagers is that they're capable of managing their emotions in healthy and productive ways. All you need is a little bit of practice.

In the following pages, I have collected useful tools and techniques to help you identify your emotions. Here you'll learn how to express your emotions in a healthy way. Sometimes that may require you to write about your feelings. In other instances, I may ask you to use different techniques such as meditation or simple drawing exercises to work through what you're feeling. The elements in this book offer a wide range of solutions so that you can find the best methods to help you experience your emotions in a healthy and productive way.

I truly believe that a life isn't measured by how smart you are, how many followers you have on social media, or any other measure of success. I believe a person's potential and eventual successes are rooted in how well they can identify and manage their emotions. That idea isn't just my own; science calls this emotional intelligence. It's the idea that our thoughts, feelings, and actions shape people more than grades, test scores, or any other measure of academic intelligence.

No matter where you live, who you live with, how you identify, what your preferred pronouns are, or what you stand for, you can be successful in life by learning to manage your emotions. You have the power to change your life when you realize your power in harnessing your emotions. Only then can you become the super-powerful driver of your life.

Let's get started!

"The best and most beautiful things in the world cannot be seen or even touched. They must be felt."

—HELEN KELLER

your emotional life

In this section, you will explore the basics of your emotions: what you feel and how you interpret that, as well as what you believe about that feeling and how you express it. You'll learn about what happens in your brain and body when you experience emotions. You'll start with the basics of emotions and move into an in-depth view of how they impact everyday life. When you are finished with this section, you'll have a stronger foundation to successfully navigate life's ups and downs.

When learning a new language, you speak in very basic vocabulary. The same goes for talking about feelings. When you're little and learning to understand your feelings, simple terms such as happy, mad, and sad are the go-to words to describe your emotions. But as you age, your emotions become much more complicated. For example, you may feel jubilant, rueful, or despondent.

To help better understand the complexities of emotions, try matching these simple emotions to a deeper emotion:

Happy	Calamitous
Mad	Reticent
Sad	Wearied
Bored	Imprudent
Lonely	Insouciant
Shy	Forlorn

People rely on simple feelings to help them through an experience. But rarely can they name the deeper emotions tied to an experience. When you can name an emotion, you can better manage it, or "name it to tame it." Think about a time you felt happy or mad or sad, and try to name three more complicated emotions that offer a more descriptive feeling. Here's an example:

WHAT I FELT	WHAT IT COULD HAVE BEEN	OR THIS	AND MAYBE EVEN THIS
Happy	Elated	Proud	Accomplished
Happy			
Mad			
Sad			

Emotions such as excitement, confidence, or gratitude are best described as comfortable to experience. Emotions such as anger, embarrassment, or worry are considered more difficult. Sometimes these emotions can fall into more than one category of happy, mad, or sad. For example, let's look at the different ways you can feel when you're embarrassed.

HAPPY: My friends all sang happy birthday to me at lunch.

MAD: My parents dropped me off at school and leaned on the horn and made everyone in the parking lot look in my direction.

SAD: My teacher called on me and I had no idea what the answer was. I felt so dumb.

How can the emotions listed here be interpreted differently? Use the previous examples for clues.

LONELY ....

....

....

HAPPY ....

....

....

MAD ....

....

....

SAD ....

....

....

....

WORRIED ....

....

....

....

SCARED ....

....

....

....

ANGRY ....

....

....

....

CONFUSED ....

....

....

Sometimes people interpret emotions differently because they have a different life experience. For example, if you grow up learning that feeling pride is rude or arrogant, you may want to keep quiet about winning a trophy. But your friend might react to winning a trophy by sharing a social media post and feeling triumphant!

Write about a time you felt differently than someone because you have a different life experience.

....

....

....

....

....

....

....

....

....

....

....

Adrian was in 10th grade when they were referred to counseling by the principal after a physical altercation at a school pep rally. Despite their annoyance with being in counseling, Adrian shared that their feelings of rage came on strong: like they boiled up, exploded, and came out of nowhere. This was Adrian's first incident of physical fighting at school. They felt guilt about hurting another student and knew they should have handled themself differently. Adrian learned that we all possess the instinctual drive to stay alive, called fight-or-flight, which occurs when our body senses danger, produces adrenaline, and responds in a very natural way. They learned that there was nothing wrong with their brain, just in their ability to handle the intensity of emotions. Adrian was able to talk through changing their actions and anger management strategies with this better understanding of human nature.

Every person expresses emotions differently. Some people can talk about feelings for hours; others don't want to talk at all! Some people would rather think, draw, doodle, or sing. How do you like to express emotions?

....

....

....

....

....

....

....

....

....

....

....

....

....

....

"For news of the heart, ask the face."

—CAMBODIAN PROVERB

Identifying Microexpressions

Humans learn to differentiate between happy, sad, and mad expressions relatively early on. But it takes much longer to master more subtle facial expressions, like surprise, fear, and disgust.

Drawing facial expressions can help you become more aware of the subtle changes in a person's face as they are experiencing feelings. Try drawing happy, mad, sad, lonely, or worried, like the emotions you see on emoji characters.

There are seven universal facial expressions, also known as microexpressions. They include anger, fear, disgust, surprise, happiness, contempt, and sadness. Microexpressions exist in every culture and are revealed in subtle changes in the lips, eyes, nose, eyebrows, and even teeth, and last from 0.5 to 4.0 seconds and cannot be faked. When you're done drawing, take some time to look in the mirror and see if you can create the seven different microexpressions. The next time you're at school, see if you identify all seven of them.

Freely writing your feelings about an experience of yours is scientifically proven to improve health, increase optimism, and build resilience. This style of writing is helpful to sort through a traumatic or scary event, or an embarrassing or uncomfortable moment. Write about a situation you recently experienced—one that you enjoyed or didn't like. Provide as much detail as you can, and don't worry about the punctuation and grammar rules you learned in language arts classes. They don't matter for this exercise.

A big piece of understanding emotions is developing a sense of who you are and what you stand for. Your personality traits, your likes and dislikes, your belief system or moral code—these are things that contribute to how you see yourself. This unique identity, or self-worth, also includes how you understand and manage your emotions. Are you always up for some fun? Do you care about your grades? Is being an elite athlete or skilled artist important to you?

What are three things you feel passionately about?

....

....

....

....

....

List three things you are proud of about yourself.

....

....

....

....

....

Have you found yourself crying tears of happiness when nothing that great happened? Have you ever felt so much anger that you slammed your bedroom door? Intense feelings are natural, but they can also come out of nowhere. Think about a time you experienced an intense emotion and write about how you felt about it.

....

....

....

....

....

....

....

....

....

....

....

....

....

....

I recently met a young student who was undergoing treatment for headaches and unexplained stomach pains. They were isolating in their room and seemed angry all the time. This student was in six AP classes, slept about three hours a night, and skipped meals often. I asked the student to identify three things they were good at, to which they replied math, organization, and hard work. But then when I asked them to identify three passions, they said being a vegetarian to save the environment, participating in an amphibian research project, and building a compost bin. This student could achieve any academic success, yet they were just going through the motions because none of their classes touched on their passions. Unfortunately, this situation is all too common. This student then began finding ways to incorporate their passions into school assignments, by writing English papers about topics they cared about and even using their upcoming compost project in science and math classes.

"Peace begins with a smile."

—MOTHER THERESA

Recognizing Smiles

Just like recognizing the seven universal facial expressions, recognizing a genuine smile, one that comes from true enjoyment, will also add to your skills in understanding and recognizing emotion. A polite smile has upturned lips. A genuine smile is said to reach the eyes. Your clues are the little wrinkles around the eyes when someone smiles at you. The next time you're talking to people and having fun, look for that genuine smile—that means they are truly comfortable and enjoying that moment.

A 2013 study by neuroscientists found that even mild levels of stress can impact a person's ability to regulate their emotions. In this study, the researchers put half of the participants under mild stress by having them hold their hand in icy water. The other half had their hand in warm, soothing water. Then they showed the participants pictures of snakes and spiders to increase their stress. The participants that were stressed by the icy water were less able to manage their fear when shown the pictures. The people with their hand in warm, soothing water could use stress management techniques and had less fear. You won't have to look at spiders and snakes, but do think about some of your biggest sources of stress and write them down.

Doing things that bring you happiness is an easy way reduce stress and worry. Feeling happy strengthens your immune system, reduces pain, and increases life expectancy. Think about what makes you happy. Perhaps it's making a playlist, binge-watching your favorite show, or getting a good grade on a test that you studied really hard for. Write down five things, people, places, or experiences that always make you happy.

Just as feeling happy is a part of life, so is feeling sad. Many people try to avoid feeling sad, but this emotion is healthy and important. When you feel sad, your mind and body are saying it's time to take a break to reevaluate what you want. Think about a recent experience that made you feel really sad.

Describe what happened.

....

....

....

....

....

....

What part contributed to you feeling sad?

....

....

....

....

....

....

Most people don't have much trouble expressing themselves when they're mad. Maybe you yell, scream, or cry. All of these are excellent expressions of feeling mad, as long as you don't hurt anybody or anything. The challenge in managing mad feelings usually comes after you express them in hurtful ways. Think about the last time you were really mad.

How did you respond? ....

....

....

....

....

....

If you could go back, would you change how you responded? ....

....

....

....

....

....

Just as you can't control the weather, you can't control other people's thoughts, feelings, or actions. At the same time, you are the only person who controls what you feel. I often hear my teenage clients express their feelings about a given situation with statements such as, "He made me so mad," or "She made me so happy." Believing that other people can sway your emotions gives away your power. Learning to be in control of your superpowered emotions frees you from other people's influence on them.

What actions or things has someone done that caused you to feel angry and/or happy? How did you express that?

Anxiety is an official mental health diagnosis, which we will explore in more detail later in this journal. Right now, I want you to get an idea of the concept of worry, which is really a reaction to a stressful or troubling situation. Here are some different words for the word "worry." Circle any that you've experienced. Feel free to write down others that you think of to describe the word.

Stress	Worry	Edgy
Jumpy	Jitters	Apprehension
Nervous	Fear	Butterflies
Uneasy	Angst	Freaking out
Panic	Agitated	

Everybody feels sad from time to time. Feeling sad about something occasionally is completely normal. Everybody has sad days and experiences. But feeling sad all the time or most of the time for at least six months could be diagnosed as depression. It's important to know when your feelings don't seem to shift. Talk to a trusted adult or seek counseling if you feel your sadness isn't lifting.

Which of these feelings best describes you when you feel depressed?

Gloomy	Melancholy	Despair
Devastation	Hopeless	Lonely
Desperate	Miserable	Discouraged

Your feelings and your thoughts get thrown together to create a picture of who you are. This is called your self-worth. This sense of self is created by feeling comfortable with many different emotions, learning about your strengths, and being proud of how you present yourself. Take some time to think about your home life, and how you express and behave toward your family.

I'm happy when my family and I

....

....

....

....

....

My family would say the best thing about me is

....

....

....

....

....

Your self-worth is also related to your life while you're at school. This can be reflected in your school work and your social life. Take a few minutes to think about how you express yourself and behave at school, toward your friends, your teachers, and the cafeteria workers.

I'm a good friend because I

....

....

....

....

....

....

My teachers would say the best thing about me is

....

....

....

....

....

The last place I want you to reflect on your self-worth is in your community. That can mean different things to different people. Perhaps you play sports, have a part-time job, a hobby, or volunteer. Take some time to think about how you express yourself and behave in your community.

I'm a good citizen because I

....

....

....

....

....

....

My coaches/mentors/neighbors would say the best thing about me is

....

....

....

....

....

The Three Pillars of Mental Wellness

If you were asked to build a tower using deck of playing cards, I bet you'd spend time creating a strong base in order to give it a solid foundation. Your emotions also need a solid foundation. For humans, that means eating a healthy diet, getting enough sleep, and exercising every day. If any of those areas are neglected, your mental and physical health won't continue to thrive in a positive way. Think about last week. How much sleep did you get each night? Did you eat three healthy meals each day? Did you get in any form of physical activity?

I bet school starts early. I'm also going to bet that you race out the door to make the first bell, so maybe breakfast is an afterthought. I know that getting up early isn't easy for teens. But it's imperative that you give your brain and body the fuel it needs to get going for that 8:00 a.m. calculus class. This week, I challenge you to eat a different mini breakfast each day. It could be a couple sticks of cheese, a yogurt, or even cold pizza. Keep track of which foods kept you full and helped you stay focused in class.

Biologically, a teen's internal clock shifts during adolescence to be up and alert later at night and less awake in the morning. That's because right now your body produces melatonin, the chemical that helps you sleep, later in the evening than it did when you were a kid. It doesn't seem right that this happens during your teenage years, when you need the most sleep! In the next few weeks, commit to getting a good night's sleep—eight hours, at least. Try each one of the routines listed here for at least three nights in a row. When you've gone through this entire list, think about which one worked best.

➡ Establish a routine for bedtime. For example, take a shower, listen to music, and then get in bed.
➡ Avoid caffeine, especially energy drinks and coffee, after 7:00 p.m.
➡ Keep your sleeping space colder than the rest of the house and as dark as possible.
➡ Most important, turn off your computer, video games, AND cell phone at least an hour before going to bed, and leave all of these devices out of your room (so you are not tempted to check just one more text!).

Exercise increases your endorphins. Scientists call these the "feel-good chemicals" that your body produces because they relieve stress and pain. You don't need to run a marathon or go pump iron in a gym to boost your endorphins. Simply find a way to move that you enjoy. Experiment with yoga or stretching. Ride a bike to meet a friend. Take your neighbor's dog for a walk. Make a commitment for the next month to do some form of exercises as least three times a week.

Your brain is a superhighway of neurons that carries messages at more than 149 miles per hour. Remember that race car we talked about earlier? These neurons aren't connected, so your body uses neurotransmitters (a chemical) to bridge that gap so messages can be carried between them. There are 40 neurotransmitters in all, but dopamine, endorphins, serotonin, and oxytocin are four of the most important.

Dopamine is the reward chemical. You get a shot of dopamine when you anticipate or do something that brings pleasure and enjoyment, such as watching a favorite video, completing something on your to-do list, or eating something delicious. What are three things you can do to boost your dopamine?

....

....

....

....

....

....

....

....

Endorphins are the "feel-good" hormones. They are produced when you laugh, exercise, or eat dark chocolate. Try all three of these at different times and notice when you feel endorphins kicking in. Write about each experience.

....

....

....

....

....

Serotonin stabilizes your mood, feelings of well-being, and happiness. It also aids in eating, sleeping, and digestion. Meditating, getting a safe amount of sun, or exercising all boost your serotonin. What are three ways you plan to boost your serotonin this week?

....

....

....

....

....

Oxytocin is the "love hormone," which is released when we snuggle up with a loved one or hang out with friends. You can increase your oxytocin by hugging someone, giving or getting compliments, or even having a thumb war. Commit to boosting your oxytocin this week and write down three different ways you plan to do so.

"But feelings can't be ignored, no matter how unjust or ungrateful they seem."

—ANNE FRANK, THE DIARY OF A YOUNG GIRL

2

expressing emotions

You learned that you must name an emotion in order to understand it. The next step is to explore the importance of expressing that emotion. Expressing emotions in a healthy way can help you form stronger connections with the people in your life, can help you be more successful at school or a job, and can help you feel heard, understood, and valued by the people in your life. Just like every person feels things differently, every person expresses emotions uniquely. However, emotions must be expressed. That is a universal truth.

Anne Frank, the young daughter of a Jewish family who hid in an upstairs apartment for over two years during the Holocaust, dealt with tremendously complicated feelings by writing in her now famous diaries. But she wasn't the first to turn to writing as a way to sort through her emotions. Now it's your turn. Write about a boring event that happened today. Your challenge is to use five feelings words, found on page 53. You can make it a paragraph or a poem, a pretend diary entry, or even a social media post!

Have you ever wanted to cry while talking with a teacher, but held the tears back? Maybe you were so mad at a friend but you didn't feel you could say anything. Ignoring your emotions isn't like holding down the brake pedal in a car. Your emotions will continue, but you won't be dealing with them in a healthy way. Write about a time when you felt a lot of emotion but tried to ignore it or stop it from happening.

Tye was referred to counseling by a teacher who said his grades had slipped to F's and that he was falling asleep in class. Tye's mom had recently been diagnosed with cancer and he would not express any emotions about this. I decided to first start with the three pillars of mental wellness for both Tye and his dad. With having mom sick, their foundation was already shaky. Tye said that they never had dinner anymore; instead, they just found food to eat, and even though people had offered to make food, they hadn't taken anyone up on it. Tye and his dad agreed to let people know they could use a dinner or two, and packed cold lunches for Tye to take to school. Through the conversations and changes, Tye was able to feel safer and more secure in knowing his dad, with the help of friends and extended family, could take care of the family. By trying to block out the **hard** emotions, like fear and worry, Tye and his dad were missing out on **all** the emotions, including support and nurturing and kindness. They both learned to take care of the basics, so they would have energy for things like work, school, and managing some pretty tough emotions.

One of easiest ways to sort out your emotions is to make a simple statement about them. An "I" statement is a good formula for identifying the emotion and describing what is triggering that feeling. For example, "I feel happy when you say you love me," or "I feel annoyed when the teacher announces a pop quiz." Now it's your turn.

I feel .... when ....

I feel .... when ....

I feel .... when ....

I feel .... when ....

I feel .... when ....

Having someone in your life who is a good listener is the best remedy to helping you sort through your emotions. Write the names of people in your life who would be good listeners. Think about what topics you feel comfortable talking about with each person.

....

....

....

....

....

....

....

....

....

....

....

....

....

....

"To shut down the ability to feel pain means you shut down all emotions, joy included."

—JEWEL, AMERICAN SINGER-SONGWRITER, MUSICIAN, ACTRESS, AND AUTHOR

Let's build on that last prompt. Take each "I" statement and fill in the first blank with words that express even deeper feelings. By extending the sentence, you will increase your ability to identify your feelings with precise language.

I feel guilty when the teacher announces a pop quiz because I know I didn't finish my readings last night.

Now it's your turn:

I feel .... when ....

because ....

I feel .... when ....

because ....

I feel .... when ....

because ....

I feel .... when ....

because ....

I feel .... when ....

because ....

Photo Expressions

Your emotions aren't just communicated through words. Body posture, eye contact, gestures, touch, and facial expressions are other ways we express ourselves. For example, a person who has their arms crossed tightly around their body is communicating their defensiveness or feeling guarded.

Go through a dozen or so photos of you and your friends on your phone. Can you pick up on the different emotions people are expressing in these images? What emotions do you see: Confidence? Openness? Sassiness? Silliness?

Eye contact is a way express emotion, to convey that you hear and respect the other person. When you make eye contact with someone, it means you are listening and that you hear and understand what the person is saying. On the other hand, a well-placed eye roll can say you don't like what a person is saying. The next time you talk to a friend and a stranger, take a minute to think about the eye contact you witness as you're talking to them. Write about the experience here.

A handshake or a high five can communicate many emotions. Your hands have the capability to "speak" in harmful or compassionate ways.

If you hold up a peace sign to a friend, what emotion do you think you'd be feeling?

....

....

....

....

....

What emotions does a negative hand gesture mean?

....

....

....

....

....

You learned earlier that certain facial expressions are understood across cultures and languages. But what about other facial expressions you make? What unique facial expressions do you make? Draw your favorite facial expression here.

Music and Emotions

Listening to music is an emotional experience. That's because certain notes and words, when in combination, invoke emotion. Look at your favorite playlist on your phone. Write down your top 10 songs and identify an emotion you feel when listening to them. Remember to go beyond happy, sad, and mad.

Emotions such as happiness and joy are usually easy and comfortable. Hard emotions such as loneliness and guilt are more difficult. No one likes to feel hard emotions but they are necessary and they will come. The key to expressing hard emotions is knowing where they come from. Think of a time you felt guilty about something.

What triggered the emotion?

....

....

....

....

....

What caused you to feel that way?

....

....

....

....

....

What were your thoughts about the emotion?

....

....

....

....

....

How did you respond or not respond to the emotion?

....

....

....

....

....

Body Scan

Emotions must be released in some way. If they aren't expressed, they can become actual pain in your body as a headache, backache, or stomachache. A body scan is a meditation technique that can help you bring focused attention to that body part and emotion. The hope is that by finding where your body carries stress, you can reduce your symptoms. Try this simple body scan.

➡ Take a few deep breaths. Breathe in slowly from your nose. Hold it and then release it slowly out of your mouth, like you are blowing out a birthday candle.

➡ While continuing to breathe slowly and rhythmically, pay attention to your feet. Think about how you feel and notice any sensations. Take another deep breath and repeat for all body parts: knees, legs, stomach, heart, arms, legs, and head. Pay attention to each body part and keep breathing slowly in and out.

➡ Scan your whole body. Did you notice tension anywhere? Were there any spots that you found yourself carrying pain or tightness?

Check out Insight Timer, Smiling Mind, and Headspace for more detailed body scans.

"Just keep swimming, just keep swimming!"

—DORY, IN *FINDING NEMO*

In *Finding Nemo,* the clownfish Dory was scared and lost. But she also had her saying that helped her get through tough situations. Dory was using a mantra to help her through stressful times. A mantra is a phrase or saying that acts like a mini meditation, which can help break up negative thoughts and bring your focus to positive thoughts. Brainstorm for a few minutes and write down phrases such as, "I can do this," "I've got this," or "tomorrow is another day" to begin creating your own personal mantra.

....

....

....

....

....

....

....

....

....

....

....

....

Creative Calming

Art is the perfect way to express your emotions, because you don't have to be skilled to create. Studies show that drawing, doodling, and coloring are calming activities and reduce feelings of worry. For this exercise you will draw and color a mandala or flower. While you color, think about what's worrying you. Take 10 minutes a day for this type of creative expression. If you need more pages to color, try a coloring book or just doodle on a piece of paper.

Ash was in eighth grade when she came to counseling with selective mutism, which is the inability to talk during periods of high stress. As you can imagine, coming to counseling to talk about not talking was pretty stressful for Ash! When we eliminated all the unintentional forms of expressing emotion, like eye contact, body posture, gestures, and facial expressions, Ash was better able to identify her own feelings. By coloring mandalas, beading bracelets, or doing intricate crafts, Ash began to see that she could identify emotions and even express them. We were able to slowly add eye contact and other nonverbal skills back to the session once she became more comfortable. Breaking down expression of feeling into tiny parts made each part more manageable for Ash. She was eventually able to order food at a restaurant and even got a job at the local humane society!

The Five Senses

Sometimes an emotion just needs to be felt. Tapping into your five senses can help you focus on your emotions. Let's try this mindfulness exercise to tap into your emotions that you're feeling right now.

➡ Take a few minutes to sit or lie down in a quiet space.

➡ What do you **see**? Is it bright, dark, clean, organized, or pretty? Focus on what you see. How do you feel?

➡ Then take a breath and focus on what you **hear**. What noise did you not notice before? What can you hear? How do you feel?

➡ Now focus again on your **touch**. Do you feel a comfortable chair, or is the floor hard on your back? Is it cold when you feel the wall?

➡ Take another deep breath. Do you **smell** anything: food, body wash, fresh air? Does smell trigger any feelings?

➡ And lastly, what do you **taste**? Can you taste a lingering piece of gum or candy, toothpaste, or saltiness? Does taste bring up feelings? Do you have happy memories of taste?

Positive and Negative Emotions

Earlier you used your natural creative expression to help you focus and calm yourself. Let's take that exercise a step further. Focus on a feeling, whether happy, mad, or sad, or something deeper, and draw whatever you feel. Try experimenting with both positive and negative emotions and see what happens.

Using what you've learned about expressing emotions, including nonverbal expression, think about how you typically express the three basic emotions—happy, mad, and sad—as you go about your daily life. Are you intentional about what you convey? The next time you're out with friends, think about your body language when they're talking to you. Do you cross your arms? How about your hands? Do you stop making eye contact? Do you give a genuine smile? Then think about these same things the next time your mom is talking to you about cleaning your room. Write about the differences here.

Try Something New

Often trying a new activity can help you explore different emotions. The same can be said for trying a physical activity, too. Think about a sport or activity that you've always been curious about but haven't tried. This can be as involved as learning to play tennis or as simple as skateboarding. This next week, make a promise to give it a try. While doing that activity, pay attention to your feelings. In the coming week, choose from one of these skills and make a commitment to noticing and practicing that skill.

⇨ Use at least three "I" statements to focus on your feelings and your observation about what is triggering the emotion. ("I" statements)

⇨ Write, draw, sing, talk, or craft it out. (Bring focused attention to the feeling to allow your mind and body to fully feel the emotion.)

⇨ Check your unintentional communication. Does it match your true emotion? (Matching intentional with unintentional behavior)

⇨ Feel your feelings. Go through your senses or do a body scan and notice. (Physical presence)

⇨ Remind yourself of your positive attributes or your mantra. (Mantra practice)

"That gnawing sense of self-doubt that is common within all of us is a lie. It's just in our heads. Nine times out of ten, we are more ready and more prepared than we could ever know."

—MICHELLE OBAMA

3

managing emotions

Even when you can identify and express emotions, they can still feel overwhelming at times. In this section, you are going to learn how to embrace your emotions and accept them, with coping skills including breath practice, becoming aware of your triggers, cognitive behavioral therapy (CBT), and radical acceptance. The goal is to give you the skills to work through and move past those emotions that hold you back or tend to trip you up in your daily life. This next part is going to be filled with challenges, but I believe you're up for it. Let's get started!

Belly Breath

Paying attention to your breathing helps you connect to your emotions. This type of practice is called focused breathing or belly breathing. Whatever you decide to call it, the exercise gives you the opportunity to notice and feel what is happening for you in each moment. It can be hard to slow down with everything happening in your life, so consider completing this exercise at the end of your day. Let's give it a try.

1. Lie down on your back, put your phone or journal on your stomach, and notice your breath.

2. Breathe in through your nose slowly and try to make your phone or journal rise up on your full belly.

3. The intake breath should allow your lungs to expand so far that your belly needs to get out of the way.

4. Your belly should rise and make that object lift up. You want your stomach to look huge!

5. Breathe in through your nose, watch your belly rise, and see how high you make it go. See how long you can hold that breath with your belly extended, then release the breath slowly, like you are blowing out a birthday candle.

6. Practice this exercise every day until you can do it sitting, standing, or in any other position. Focus on your lungs filling fully and then releasing that breath completely.

Once you get the hang of belly or focused breathing, the next step toward mastering your emotions is to think how you're feeling during the exercise. Practice steps 1 through 5 from page 60. But this time as you're breathing, pay attention to how your inhale and exhale make you feel. Just like you learned in the prompt about naming your emotions (page 3), notice how you feel, both physically and emotionally. Circle any of these feelings or sensations you feel while practicing a belly breath and use the lines to write in anything else that you felt.

Sleepy   Slowed breathing   Tingly

Relaxed   Relieved   Light-headed

Stiff   Calm   Peaceful

Slowed heart rate

....

....

....

....

....

....

Positive Thoughts and Images

Now let's introduce positive feelings or images to your belly breath exercise. This could be a favorite place you have vacationed, a person who is always happy to see you, or even a few lines from a song you love. Once you have your place, person, or thing in mind, sit quietly and practice steps 1 through 5 from page 60. Now focus on your positive thought. How does it feel? Do you notice a sense of calm or peacefulness?

Developing a saying to use during your belly breath practice can also help reduce stress. Similar to the mantras you created on page 50, this mantra is about creating calm as you practice focused breathing. Come up with one for the inhale, such as, "I breathe in calm and breathe out negativity," and one for the exhale, such as, "I breathe in peace and breathe out love." Think about what words or phrases will help you feel calm as you practice belly breathing.

Deep Breathing

Now that you've learned how to practice belly breaths and you have your breath mantras and your visualization, let's bring it all together with one final element—intentionally forcing out air through your mouth in a slow and careful manner. Think of this step as blowing out a birthday candle in a very long, slow breath. It's a super stress reliever. Practice steps 1 through 5 from page 60, remembering your mantras from page 50. But as you repeat the steps this time, once your lungs are fully inflated and your belly is huge, breathe out all the air in a loud and forceful manner.

Emotional Clues

Often feelings show up in your body before you fully recognize the emotion. Think for a minute about the last time you were overwhelmed with anger. Did your mind go blank? Did your face turn red? Did your heart race? If you can't recall a previous time, keep this prompt in mind the next time your body starts to react to an experience that makes you upset.

When unwanted feelings are triggered—by people, events, or experiences—your brain will make up a reason for your reaction. This is all part of human nature; your brain wants to justify the reaction, even if it doesn't make sense. An example would be when you are scrolling on social media and you see a post of your BFF hanging out with someone else. You may feel sad, jealous, or angry. Your brain tries to justify that feeling, so perhaps you think that your BFF doesn't really like you. Seeing that post triggered feelings of jealousy and loneliness. Circle any of these common triggers you have felt.

Feeling rejected

Feeling betrayed

Believing you are being treated unfairly

Someone challenges you or your passions

Feeling helpless or out of control

Being left out

Not being given space or the independence desired

Feeling unloved, unwanted, or unworthy

Feeling criticized

Unwanted feelings are emotions that you don't want to experience because they're uncomfortable or painful. But unwanted feelings give you an opportunity to manage your emotions. One of the best ways to practice managing your emotions is by mentally stepping outside of the experience as it happens. That doesn't mean you stop feeling. But you can teach yourself to take a moment and think about why you're feeling a certain way instead of just acting on it. Think of a time, person, event, or something else that triggered emotions in you recently. What did it trigger? What came up for you? Can you trace the emotion back to the experience?

When humans are faced with danger, the body is designed to go into fight-or-flight mode. It is an instinctual drive to literally stay alive! Your brain identifies danger and flips into survival mode by producing a chemical called adrenaline. The adrenaline sends signals throughout the body that result in super speed, strength, and awareness. In a real situation of danger, this would allow you to fight (deal with the problem) or flight (flee the problem), and either way would use up that adrenaline. It is a great design!

   Think about would you do if you were being chased by a woolly mammoth. (Fight? Run? Not sure?) What about if a fire started in your kitchen? (Get out fast? Put out the fire? Not sure?)

Now that you have a general idea of what fight-or-flight means, let's apply it to a time from your own life. Think about a time when you went into survival mode and made the decision to fight. Have you ever? Or would you rather flee? Be specific.

....

....

....

....

....

....

....

....

....

....

....

....

....

....

....

....

What about a time when your survival mode kicked in and you decided to flee a situation. Have you ever? Or would you rather fight? Spare no details.

_____

_____

_____

_____

_____

_____

_____

_____

_____

_____

_____

_____

_____

_____

_____

Finally, write about a time when you felt that adrenaline surge but didn't need it after all. Perhaps it was something minor or a close call, but nothing threatening. Did you notice the adrenaline rush without having done something about it?

Kai was terrified of bees, so much so that going out the front door of the house was no longer an option, because somewhere out there was a beehive. Kai would scream if a bee was spotted or heard. Kai learned that the thought of a bee triggered a panic response. Her brain had created a powerful connection between a bee and something else. Through talking, visualizing, belly breathing, and learning about triggers, Kai discovered the connection. Years earlier when Kai was small, a bee got in the car as the family was driving and Kai's dad was screaming, swearing, and driving erratically. Seeing her dad out of control, Kai felt scared and terrified. Seeing or hearing a bee would trigger all those feelings of "out of control" again for Kai.

Adrenaline Energy

If you have too much adrenaline pumping through your body—because your brain sensed danger and you produced too much adrenaline, but you didn't need it after all—it can feel like your chest is tightening or your body is shaking. Quick bursts of exercise can use it all up, such as one minute of burpees or jumping jacks. Think about three other ways for you to use up your adrenaline by exercising, and remember it next time you have some adrenaline to burn.

"If you don't like something, change it. If you can't change it, change your attitude."

—MAYA ANGELOU

Radical acceptance is about acknowledging when a situation is out of your control and fully accepting it. Let's say you had plans to go the movies with friends, but now it's snowing, and your mom doesn't want to drive you anywhere and she doesn't want you to take the bus in bad weather. A more upsetting situation would be if your best friend moved to another state. You can acknowledge how hurt you feel, but then work hard to accept it as a change that is uncomfortable but not in your control. Which statements of radical acceptance do you find yourself drawn to:

☐ This is the way it has to be for now.

☐ I hate this, but I have to deal with it.

☐ I'm a good friend and someone else will like me.

☐ This moment will pass.

☐ I can't control other people.

Radical acceptance is less about ignoring what is difficult and more about accepting that the situation is hard—and sometimes unbearably hard. Radical acceptance might come in handy when someone breaks up with you, seemingly out of nowhere. You can't control their interest in you, but you can control how you respond. During these painful moments, scenes from your favorite movies or TV shows, or a favorite song can come in handy. Thinking about the lines from songs, movies, or TV shows that you really enjoy can help you accept a situation you can't control.

Although it's always good to acknowledge your emotions, sometimes a good approach to managing your feelings is to think in opposites. If you feel angry, listen to calming music. If you feel agitated, take a soothing bath. If you feel sad, watch funny videos.

What will you try the next time you have a difficult emotion? Think of a few action items that you can turn to when you feel overwhelmingly sad, stressed, or angry.

Purposeful Distraction

The idea of distraction sometimes get a bad reputation. You've probably heard "pay attention and stop being so distracted" from your family or teachers. But distraction can actually help you manage emotions if used purposefully. Spending hours on YouTube because you don't want to study for your geometry test isn't going to make your stress go away. But using *purposeful* distraction, such as listening to music, creating art, or baking can help you overcome the original emotion. Over the next week, prepare to practice purposeful distraction. Lay out art supplies, bookmark a new cookie recipe, or make a playlist of songs.

When you feel thirsty, you drink. When you are hungry, you eat. You feel sad, so you isolate. You feel mad, so you yell. Every emotion is followed by an action. By choosing a different action, you can also change the original feeling. By acting the way you want to feel, you can change that feeling.

Feeling sad? What action do you want to take? Cry, hide in your room, or listen to sad music? What opposite action can you take to change the sadness?

....

....

....

....

....

....

Feeling mad? What action do you tend to take? Do you yell, scream, cry, or hang out in your room alone? What opposite action can you take?

....

....

....

....

....

....

"Crying helps me slow down
and obsess over the
weight of life's problems."

−SADNESS, FROM INSIDE OUT

Crying is a great way to express sadness, because it provides a physical release and can make you feel more settled and calm. Think about the last time your cried. Was is because you were sad or happy? Did you get yelled at by someone? Did you fail your driver's test? Write about it here.

Kaden came to counseling a few years after her dad died. She talked about feeling sad all the time. Her grandma said that Kaden was spending more time in her room and on her phone. Through counseling, Kaden was better able to identify that she felt sad but also really mad, disappointed, and lonely without her dad. By identifying these deeper feelings, Kaden was able to accept the heaviness of this situation, which is the radical acceptance we already discussed. And although she can't change her dad's death, she found that listening to music he used to listen to comforted her and helped her feel lighter and happier. She found that when she felt most sad or mad, by taking a different action, such as coming out of her room and doing purposefully distracting things, she felt less alone, too. She baked cookies with her grandma and she even learned to crochet a scarf! Kaden was able to change her feelings of deep sadness, anger, and loneliness to sad, connected, and proud.

Creating a Plan

Kaden's story is a good example of life getting complicated. She was faced with a terrible loss. She wasn't prepared to deal with so many emotions at one time. One way to be better prepared for both the big losses in life and also the really small ones, such as losing your favorite sunglasses in the lake, is to create a plan for when you will experience both the big and the small struggles. Take a look at the following list. Answer the questions as honestly as you can.

RADICAL ACCEPTANCE

What is the hard feeling? Why is it happening? Can you control it?

SELF-SOOTHING

What things bring you calm? What activities or behaviors do you find soothing?

DISTRACTION

What purposeful distraction can you try?

OPPOSITE ACTION

What is an opposite action for your feelings?

As you learned earlier in this journal, becoming aware of what you're feeling and why you're feeling it makes it easier to manage your emotions in any situation. Scientists call this emotional intelligence, or EI. A big part of EI is showing yourself compassion through positive self-talk. To boost your positive inner voice, start by answering these statements:

My best characteristic is ....

....

I am my most happy when ....

....

I am the best version of me when ....

....

I love this about myself ....

....

I can give others this ....

....

"You yourself, as much as anybody
in the entire universe,
deserve your love and affection."

—BUDDHA

Improve Your Self Talk

Thoughts can create feelings, and feelings can create thoughts. If you think you look gross in a new pair of jeans, you will likely feel sad, disappointed, embarrassed, or angry. At the same time, if you feel crabby, tired, and overwhelmed, you may be more likely to think your jeans look gross. One thought can lead to the other. The next time you experience negative self-talk, use this formula of feelings, thoughts, and actions to change your tone with yourself.

➡ What am I feeling?
➡ What are my thoughts right now?
➡ How am I acting right now?

"So, the first step in seeking happiness is learning. We first have to learn how negative emotions and behaviors are harmful to us and how positive emotions are helpful."

—DALAI LAMA

4

conquering negativity

To combat sad, mad, or even bad emotions, humans have a funny way of dealing with these intense and overwhelming experiences. Think for a minute about what you tell yourself when you experience negative feelings. Maybe you think you'll never be good enough or will always be left out. Maybe you think things will never change. I'll let you in on a secret. That's your brain working overtime to make your difficult feelings less painful. I call them thought errors, and they brush aside your feelings so you don't have to truly deal with them.

In this section, you'll be introduced to the different ways your brain thinks when justifying negative emotions. You'll explore new methods to identify what you're REALLY feeling and learn new tricks and techniques to deal with emotions in a healthy way—long after your teen years are gone.

One of the most common thought errors that people use is something called all-or-nothing thinking. This can be a declaration that life is perfect or going wrong. When negative emotions come up, teens tend to fall back on negative thought errors. A situation is a complete disaster, or a total failure. The truth is, life's experiences are more nuanced than we tend to believe. Think about a time you relied on negative thought errors to cope with difficult emotions. Maybe it had to do with a bad grade on your biology midterm. Maybe your boyfriend broke up with you, or you and your best friend got into a fight and didn't talk for days.

Compassion is a great tool to help silence that all-or-nothing feeling. Compassion allows you to be kind and considerate by giving you the space to make mistakes or change your mind or reevaluate what's important. Instead of thinking, "I didn't do my homework, so I'm going to fail science this year," a compassionate thought would be, "I had hoped to get caught up on science labs, but life got overwhelming, so I'll have to try again tomorrow."

Compassion is a big fan of the middle ground. It takes away the black-and-white thinking and presents the possibility of gray. Using the same memories from the previous prompt, imagine your friend telling you that same story. What would you tell that person to make them feel better? How would you approach a friend in the same situation? Write your compassionate response here.

Let's say your friend's boyfriend broke up with them right after school, but you had to get to Robotics Club and prep for an upcoming competition. Using a rating scale of 0 to 100, what kind of friend would that make you? Zero means you ignored your friend after school and sneaked away, and 100 means you bailed on Robotics Club to let your friend cry on your shoulder. Now think about time when you were faced with a similar situation. What would have defined zero on your scale? What would have defined 100? Where did you land?

Negative self-talk is the perfect method to set yourself up for disappointment. Often negative self-talk begins with words such as, "I should," "I have to," or "I need to." The word "should" implies you can do more or better or different, which isn't always a bad thing. But it can also indicate, "I can't," "I won't," or "I didn't." Using "should" keeps yourself feeling as if nothing is going your way, which can ultimately lead to feelings of jealousy, disappointment, embarrassment, or shame. Write down three "I should," "I have to," or "I need to" statements that you used in the past week and look for any patterns for when they appear.

Compassionate self-talk plays a huge role in breaking you out of the all-or-nothing way of thinking. Every time you find yourself using a "should" statement, try using a softer approach, such as, "It would be nice if . . ." or "Eating healthy is so hard to do when I'm so busy, I will try to add more vegetables to my day." Read the following sentences and reframe the statements so they're more compassionate.

I should really work out every day.

....

....

....

....

I should try harder to look nice for school.

....

....

....

....

I should be a better friend!

....

....

....

....

Taking complicated feelings from a particularly challenging experience and applying them to other situations is called overgeneralizing. This is when people take their feelings from an experience and allow themselves to be defined by single situation or interaction.

A low grade on an English paper means you aren't a good writer.

When in reality, maybe you didn't do as well as you might have liked on this paper because you didn't prepare enough—this time. Now it's your turn. Think about a situation that didn't turn out as you expected and you overgeneralized your feelings about the outcome. What triggered you to come to that conclusion? Be sure to capture the moment and all the emotions you experienced.

....

....

....

....

....

....

....

....

....

....

Track Your Self Talk

Did you use any of these words in your description of a time you overgeneralized: always, never, everybody, nobody? During the next week, pay attention to your self-talk and notice if you find yourself using those words. Use your phone to keep track. Give yourself a smiley face when you catch yourself and change your wording.

Have you ever thought that your friends were mad at you because no one answered your text? That's called catastrophizing! It's when your feelings leave you with a worst-case scenario. An easy way to avoid catastrophizing is to use facts instead of fiction to check your thinking. Ask yourself if this information is true and proven.

So, no one answered on the group chat.
(TRUE)

Everyone hates me.
(UNPROVEN)

There could be a logical explanation.
(TRUE)

They could all be busy.
(TRUE)

So, let's look at the example from the previous prompts.

A low grade on an English paper means you aren't a good writer.

Use facts or truths to check your thinking. What could you say to yourself to ensure you are sticking with only proven truths?

....

....

....

....

....

....

....

....

....

....

....

....

....

....

Remember Adrian, the student who got in the fight and was relieved to learn that the anger was coming from their intense feelings? Adrian was quick to view their situation in all-or-nothing terms. In that situation, as soon as the first punch was thrown, they were certain that the future included being expelled, thrown in juvenile detention, and any hopes of attending college were over! Once Adrian was able to take a deep breath and talk it through, it became clearer that this specific situation was not good, but that it didn't define the entire future. Adrian had to learn to challenge their thinking that things were all or nothing by eliminating the words "always" and "never" when thinking or talking about their situation. Adrian also used a scale of 1 to 100 to continually check the severity of things when new information came out, like after talking with the principal. Instead of each new event triggering feelings of hopelessness, Adrian was able to move the scale a bit one way or the other and see that the situation was constantly changing and could continue to change. This gave them hope.

Perfectionism is the belief that you must always be right or good or the best at anything and everything you do. People who are perfectionists tend to take fewer risks because the thought of not being perfect at something holds them back. The truth is, no one is perfect and holding yourself to that standard is sure to lead to disappointment and failure. Motivation and hard work are great. But if your motivation and drive crosses into negative self-talk, your self-worth will suffer. Write about a time when you demanded perfection from yourself. Perhaps it was an after-school performance or during a game.

....

....

....

....

....

....

....

....

....

....

....

....

Negative self-talk can be shut down through self-compassion. Instead of treating yourself with a different standard than what you hold everyone else to, embrace a single standard for everyone including yourself. Give yourself the same encouragement that you would a trusted friend.

When you haven't met the high standard you set for yourself, what do you find yourself thinking to yourself? Let's say you got your standardized test back and you got a lower score than you wanted. Your friend got the same test back with the same lower-than-desired score. What would you say to her?

....

....

....

....

....

Now say that same thing to yourself.

....

....

....

....

....

Personalization is when you center yourself as the reason that a specific action is taking place, even though that action may not be about you at all. For example, if your friends couldn't hang out at your last-minute request, personalization makes you think that your friends must not like you. But the reality is that you really don't know the answer, because you don't have access to their thoughts. The good thing is that you can teach yourself to adjust your thought process. Think about a time when you personalized an unfortunate experience.

Now think about what else the outcome could've been and write down your answers here.

....

....

....

....

....

....

....

....

....

....

....

When difficult emotions such as jealousy or loneliness come up, people have a tendency to look at what is wrong and give that emotion an extreme thought to help explain it away. This is called emotional reasoning. In other words, your emotions overtake your thinking and convince you that what you're feeling is "emotionally true," even if it's not.

I feel jealous, so I must be an untrusting person.

I feel a lot of conflicting emotions, so I must be unstable.

My feelings get hurt so easily so I'm too sensative.

Think about some of the things you tell yourself when difficult emotions come up for you.

....

....

....

....

....

....

....

....

Sometimes you just have feelings. Now that you have an idea of some of the things you tell yourself when difficult emotions, let's work on correcting this emotional reasoning.

Go back to the exercise (page 86) Improve Your Self Talk and review the formula of feelings, thoughts, and actions.

Now using your example from the previous page, ask yourself:

"What was I really feeling?"

....

....

....

....

....

....

....

....

....

Now ask yourself:

"What were my thoughts?"

....

....

....

....

....

....

Now ask yourself:

"What action did I take?"

....

....

....

....

....

....

Filtering is when you focus on part of a situation and overlook the other parts. For example, your dad says you did a good job cutting the lawn but then tells you that you ruined the plants that border the lawn because you ran over them. All you heard was that you ruined the plants.

Think about a time you had feedback that was both negative and positive. What was the positive moment that you didn't recognize at the time?

What negative feedback did you focus on?

Comparing yourself to others is a very common habit for teens. You may think someone has a better body or personality or is prettier. Becoming aware of how much your own thoughts about comparisons contribute to your insecurities can make a big difference.

What comparisons do you tend to make? Are they about academic success, body image, money, or objects?

....

....

....

....

....

What feelings do you have when you start those comparisons? How do you identify jealousy? How about insecurity? Or inadequacies? Unworthiness? Or maybe even anger, because it feels unfair?

....

....

....

....

....

Cognitive behavioral therapy (CBT) teaches an idea called cognitive restructuring, which is a fancy way of saying you can change the way you think. CBT shows that when you replace an older, repeated negative thought with a more accurate or less extreme thought, you're actually training those billions of neurons (that we talked about on page 29) to take new pathways in your brain. That redirection creates a stronger likelihood that the healthier thoughts become automatic. The next time you find yourself stuck in a negative thought, use this tool to try to check it and replace it.

NOTICE THE NEGATIVE THOUGHT.

Example: *Ugh!! I hate my feet. They are so huge! I look like an elephant in these shoes!*

CHECK THE THOUGHT FOR ACCURACY. ASK YOURSELF IF IT'S TRUE.

Example: *Do my feet actually look like elephant feet? Are they really gray and 19 inches in width?* (Probably not.)

REPLACE THE NEGATIVE THOUGHT WITH A NEW, LESS EXAGGERATED THOUGHT.

Example: *My feet are bigger than average-size feet.*

Catching Errors in Thinking

You've learned about the different ways your brain can have errors in thinking that lead to complicated feelings—including catastrophizing, personalization, and emotional reasoning. Which of these ways of thinking sounds the most like you? Which one do you think you experience the most? This coming week, pay attention to the specific error in thinking that sounded most like you. Keep track of when you catch yourself thinking it and what situations you are in when it shows up the most.

"Don't carry your mistakes around with you. Instead, place them under your feet and use them as stepping stones to rise above them."

—ANONYMOUS

S. T. O. P. Negative Thoughts

Thought stopping is another useful method to halt intrusive thoughts. It's a little silly, but you literally shout the word "STOP" out loud when you notice a negative or intrusive thought. In this instance, the word is more than a command; it's also a technique to quickly tap your brain into processing your thoughts.

S Stop—Literally stop the thought to give yourself space to understand it better.

T Take a breath—Remember belly breathing? Take one of those.

O Observe—What are you feeling? Thinking? What actions are you taking?

P Proceed—You have likely changed a feeling, thought, or action, and can now proceed differently.

The next time you notice yourself experiencing a negative or intrusive thought, tell yourself to STOP.

Nadine struggled every day at middle school. She said that she ate lunch alone and no one liked her. She talked about times when someone bumped her in the hall on purpose or other students wouldn't pick her for group work so she'd have to partner with the teacher. While those are terrifying situations for any middle school student, Nadine seemed to struggle with every thought distortion. She believed her thoughts and felt lonely and isolated. Nadine could not change other people's opinions of her. She could not make others like her. But she could choose to believe that she is valuable and worthy. Through using the STOP technique, Nadine was able to identify her thought distortions and change her behaviors. By naming the thoughts, she was better able to understand her feelings and ultimately change her actions. We started with naming those distortions in therapy when she would talk about events of the week. Eventually Nadine was able to recognize some thought distortions on her own during the week. Then Nadine was able to carry herself with more confidence and begin to make friends at school.

A University of Arizona study found that people speak about 16,000 words a day to themselves in their head. It's important that those phrases be positive. After all, your inner voice shapes what you believe about yourself. It creates your self-worth, the big picture of who you are, and what you stand for! For example:

Every day is a fresh start.

Life is tough, but so am I.

I am enough.

Write down five different phrases that define your self-worth.

....

....

....

....

....

....

....

....

....

....

Practicing Empathy

Empathy is the ability to understand what other people are feeling. It's the expression of recognizing another person's experience. To practice empathy, you must first build empathy. That's as simple as talking to someone, actively listening, and asking questions. It involves having genuine curiosity about someone else and how they live their lives. In the next week, seek out someone either at home or in your school. Act like you're interviewing them for a story. Find out what things they like and don't like. Take an interest in one of their hobbies. Figure out their passions. What things do they feel most sad about in their lives? What brings them true happiness? Talk with them with an open mind and a genuine curiosity about them.

Recognizing when a thought is taking over your thinking is one of the healthiest ways to deal with your emotions. This is also known as intrusive thoughts. For example, when you are scrolling on social media and complain to yourself that you'll never have that many friends or be as good-looking as the people you follow, there is no room to feel good and happy about yourself. Creating a list of positive thoughts that you can turn to in an instant can help. Spend a few minutes writing down positive statements about yourself to counter the intrusive thoughts you experience when you scroll through social media. The next time you start to have negative thoughts, use this list to help you reframe your thinking. Remember, you want to be the driver in your race-car mind, not the passenger.

Get Ready to F.A.I.L.

Working your way through this journal won't make you perfect at managing emotions. Emotions are perfectly imperfect! You might have a day when you just need to have a good cry, or you want to be angry at the world. That is okay. Feel the feels and when you are ready, try using the acronym FAIL.

F Feel—Name it to tame it. What do you feel?

A Always keep going—What is your mantra? What makes you great? What is your self-worth?

I Insight—What thoughts and actions came along with this feeling?

L Learn—What did you learn from your rough day? What good came of the failure?

This week, watch for a time you failed to manage an emotion. Then work through the FAIL formula to better understand what happened and how you can do it differently next time.

"Being grateful all the time isn't easy. But it's when you least feel thankful that you are most in need of what gratitude can give you: perspective. Gratitude can transform any situation. It alters your vibration, moving you from negative energy to positive. It's the quickest, easiest, most powerful way to effect change in your life—this I know for sure."

—OPRAH WINFREY

Feeling Grateful

Psychologists have found that feeling grateful boosts happiness and improves psychological health over time. Studies have shown that practicing gratitude slows and discourages negative thoughts or emotions. Reminding yourself of the things you feel grateful for is a good way to boost your emotional health. I like to have teens design a personalized sun, star, or rainbow (or whatever shape you like) with words and images written in it that they come up with. This can serve as a gentle reminder of all the things you are grateful for, even when you might not be feeling it! Then you can put this up in your room, post it on social media, or just use it as a background image on your phone. Try this for yourself!

"The greatest glory in living lies not in never falling, but in rising every time we fall."

—NELSON MANDELA

5

harnessing emotions for growth

Identifying, expressing, managing, and conquering emotions is the key to living a life full of meaningful relationships and one that can handle the ups and downs of being human. After working through the exercises and writing prompts in this journal, you now have the training and the skills to deal with your emotions. Now put it all into practice! This section will give you concrete tools, tips, and reminders to keep gaining experience and the confidence to manage anything that comes your way!

A Daily Practice for Feeling Grateful

You have the power to start your day in a positive and fulfilling way. In the few minutes between waking up and getting out of bed, you have a complete fresh start. You won't be able to control your day, how others respond to you, or the things you have to do, but you can control the tone you set for the day. A daily morning practice of expressing what you're grateful for, what your intention is for the day, and how you plan to nourish yourself so you can achieve your goals will help you feel relaxed, determined, happy—and ready to take on the day.

Tomorrow morning, start your day by answering this simple question: What am I grateful for? It could be anything. Maybe you're grateful to have a family that loves you. Maybe you're grateful for having great hair, or that your biology teacher is out sick so the test is canceled.

....

....

....

....

....

....

Once you've listed what you're grateful for, now write three intentions for the day. For example: I will use my mantra today to get through the math test. I will fight hard against negative thought patterns. I intend to get my big project done.

....

....

....

....

....

....

And finally, think for a bit about what fuels you each day. Nourishment can be food for breakfast, but it can also be things or thoughts that fill you up emotionally. Maybe it's a hot shower, your favorite playlist, or a good-morning Snap to your best friend. Write down three things that nourish you in the morning.

"You've gotta believe in yourself, you just have to work harder at it than you've ever worked at anything before in your life. And if you keep doing that and believing in yourself, great things do happen."

—KATE McKINNON

Who are you? You are uniquely you! In order to be grateful, intentional, and find nourishment in life, you have to know who you are and what you stand for. What are your likes and dislikes? What are your hopes and dreams? What are your passions and interests? Who do you want to be? These questions are not to be answered once and then checked off a list. Figuring out who you truly are is a lifetime process. You will grow and change and learn new things. You will always be a work in progress.

....

....

....

....

....

....

....

....

....

....

....

....

....

Your past sets the tone for your future. You either want more of what you've had or you might be inspired to do things very differently. What has been your best accomplishment so far? What is one thing you wish you could change about your past?

....

....

....

....

....

....

....

....

....

....

....

....

....

....

Your future is what gives you hope and dreams. Having positive thoughts and feelings about your future will help you take the actions needed to get there. Those positive thoughts and feelings can also help keep you on track when life throws you a tight turn and you feel a little out of control.

What would be a really fun goal you want to accomplish in the next five years?

....

....

....

....

....

....

How will you feel when you accomplish that goal?

....

....

....

....

....

....

Wisdom is a hard concept to define, but it means having knowledge, experience, skills, and a deep understanding of something. It also involves a tolerance for tough circumstances and an ability to manage emotions, like the tools we are talking about in this journal. Pretend you are older and wiser. What piece of advice would you give to a kid at your old elementary school?

....

....

....

....

....

....

....

....

....

....

....

....

....

....

Being able to see the big picture of a situation and of your feelings can help you navigate some tough situations. How you feel right now matters. But it will change. Looking ahead to your future, what do you see? What is important for you to know about your future? To have career success, lots of friends, or to travel the world? Maybe all of it? Write about what you think your future looks like, no matter what feelings come each day.

As you work on figuring out who you are, you will make mistakes. No one finds themselves without taking a few wrong turns. Making mistakes is a part of the process. When you do make a mistake, ask yourself these questions to grow and learn. Think of a mistake you made today.

Did you say or do something that you are not proud of? What part of the mistake hurt you the most?

....

....

....

Are you still loved by your people even though you messed up? Are you still a person of value?

....

....

....

Could you have asked for help anywhere along the way to this mistake?

....

....

....

Admitting the truth when you make a mistake can be one of the most difficult things for people to do. But admitting the truth allows you to really get to know yourself in a way that no other experience can offer. Think about that same mistake from the previous prompt.

How were you honest with yourself or someone else about your mistake?

....

....

....

Why were you unable to be honest?

....

....

....

What would you do differently next time?

....

....

....

Learning to communicate your thoughts and feelings effectively will help you better manage your own emotions and help you understand other peoples' emotions. There are three styles of communication.

PASSIVE COMMUNICATION:
Too nice, powerless, not getting your wants and needs met

AGGRESSIVE COMMUNICATION:
Manipulative, hostile, arrogant

ASSERTIVE COMMUNICATION:
"I" statements, powerful, respectful

Take a moment to think about these different styles of communication. Do you find yourself relying on one of these more than the other? Do you avoid any of these? What's your comfort level with these different ways of communicating?

It's good to practice these different styles of communication, because you'll end up needing all of them as you go through life. Let's say you're in the library at school and you and your friends are starting to giggle really loud. The librarian comes over several times and says if you can't be quiet you will have to leave. Write down your different responses. Circle the one you think is the most respective and effective way to respond.

What would be a passive response?

....

....

....

....

....

....

....

....

....

What about an aggressive response?

....

....

....

....

....

....

What would be an assertive response?

....

....

....

....

....

....

Zane came to counseling during his junior year of high school. Zane hated that he would blush so deeply whenever he was in a situation where he was nervous or unsure, like being called on in class or giving a presentation. He said he couldn't even think about having a crush on someone because he was afraid that he would blush just walking by them in the hallway at school! People had teased Zane for years about his blushing and it had gotten to the point where he just stopped putting himself in any situation where he might blush. He felt powerless and always holding his emotions in. When he learned about the different communication styles and how he could use assertiveness to deal with others' criticism of him. "Yeah, I'm an open book. My face will never let me win a poker game!" His favorite line was "My body is sensing a threat from you so my adrenaline is in go mode!" That response usually got people thinking about their own behavior and caught them off guard for just enough time for Zane to regain control over the topic and feel positive about his response.

Think about a situation that causes you some embarrassment or uncomfortable feelings. Maybe you said the wrong word in class and got teased after school? Try writing down three different responses you could use: one passive, one aggressive, and one assertive.

Creating an Eco-Map

An eco-map is a tool used to draw a picture of your relationships and things that are important to you. It's often used by therapists to see who you are and how you interact with the people and things that matter to you. This helps both you and the therapist better understand how you communicate your feelings and who you have in your life to help navigate your emotional life.

Start with a circle in the center of the page. Write your name in the center. Now draw about eight smaller circles around the outside of that circle. In each smaller circle, write the name of people and things that matter to you. These can be broad categories like family, friends, sports, or school. Or you can be much more specific and put your mom in one circle and your brother in a different circle.

A Self-Care Plan

Let's jump right into the next exercise: a self-care plan. In the first column, write down the names of all the people who support you: your parents, your best friend, etc. In the last column, list all the ways you want to feel, such as happy and carefree. In between those columns, write or draw the ways you plan to take care of your emotional health, like exercising or sleeping eight hours a night. Be sure to take a picture of this plan and keep it on your phone.

People who support me	My plan	How I want to feel

Using Your Emotional Momentum

In physics, momentum is measured by how much *something* is moving and how fast it is moving. An object gains speed based on how heavy it is and how fast it can get moving.

MASS X VELOCITY = MOMENTUM

The same could be said for your feelings and emotions. But your thoughts, feelings, and actions can influence your emotional state or momentum.

THOUGHTS X FEELINGS X ACTIONS = EMOTIONAL MOMENTUM

Use this idea the next time you experience positive emotions, to keep that feeling going. You can also use it to recognize when you're spiraling down emotionally, so you can get back on track. Go for a walk or say positive things to yourself to change the momentum. These types of actions can begin to take hold and change your spiral to an upward direction!

Maintaining Positive Momentum

This week, think about the times you built on something positive. Think about small feelings, thoughts, or actions and how they have spurred more positive thoughts, feelings, and actions. Did you go for a walk and feel better? Did you text a friend and that led to the friend coming over to hang out, which led to the two of you watching a movie? What small things happened this week that kept the positive momentum going? Now think about a time when the opposite happened. Was there a time when you had a negative thought about yourself and it led to negative feelings or even self-destructive actions? Notice the times you either kept the positive momentum going or you noticed the negative momentum continuing.

What you choose to focus on will grow. Scholars call this the Law of Attraction. It's when you imagine your wish, maintain positivity, meditate about the change you want to see, write it all down, and show gratitude. By thinking, feeling, and acting in ways that are positive and focused on the person you want to be, you can become that person.

Imagine your wish. What do you want to improve upon emotionally? Feeling more confident in your body? Being with people who get you? Take a few minutes to imagine what life would look like when you achieve this goal. Brainstorm about your vision here. Write about the first thoughts that come to mind—no need to make it sound cohesive, just allow the words to flow and write.

....

....

....

....

....

....

....

....

....

....

....

Maintaining positivity is essential to your mental health. Maybe you want to have deeper friendships. Try to reframe that wish as joining more after-school activities that interest you, so you can get to know more like-minded people. How can you rephrase your wish?

A Simple Meditation

Meditate about the change you want to see. Think about the change you want and go through your five senses to think about how each sense would be affected if your vision happened to fail. Would things sound different? Would things smell different? Getting in touch with your five senses is a simple meditation you can use in any situation. What is one sense that you can relate to your goal?

Now is the time to write down all that you envisioned during your meditation. Take all those initial thoughts and visions and put them into words. What are the feelings related to the goal you have for yourself? Write down what you want to happen.

This last prompt is about gratitude. Write about three things you're grateful for. Be as specific as you can be. For example, if your wish is to have more meaningful friendships, you may say, "I'm grateful I have a few good friends. I am grateful my one friend is a good listener. I am grateful I have the opportunity to join a new club." What specific thing you're grateful for can you focus on now that you have a clear idea of the change you want to see?

....

....

....

....

....

....

....

....

....

....

....

....

....

We touched on self-care earlier and now we're going to dig a little deeper into the concept. Finding your favorite self-care activities can take some time. Start by paying attention to your likes. Do you have a hobby that you really love? Do you enjoy reading? Listening to music? Here is a list of things to get you going. Circle five of these activities that sound interesting to you. Feel free to write in other ideas, too!

Text a friend about a funny subject	Listen to a favorite song
Sit quietly and do nothing	Belly breathe
Say your mantra	Yoga
Craft	Bake
Draw	Cook
Write	Clean
Color	Read a book for fun
Scribble	Call someone
Watch a funny/cute video	Take a bath

Self-Care in Action

For the next week, challenge yourself to spend five minutes a day on the areas of self-care that you circled. Commit to doing three separate five-minute activities a day for one week. Use the following chart to write down the notes of what you did, what time of day it was, and how it felt. After a week of recording different activities at different times of the day, you may be able to find a pattern and a favorite activity!

Self-care activity	Time of day	How it felt

IKEA set up an experiment in a school's science lab. They took two identical plants and gave them the same access to sun, water, and air quality. Students complimented one plant by saying nice things to it in a soothing voice, sending it positive, loving thoughts. The students were instructed to bully the second plant. They said mean things and made faces at the plant. After 30 days, the complimented plant was growing and healthy. The bullied plant was wilted and droopy. While this experiment was admittedly not the most scientific, it is still a great concept. Imagine if you only spoke kind, loving things to yourself? And imagine how different a person you would be if you only heard mean, negative things about yourself. The lesson is to speak kindly. Believe in yourself. Use your new skills and experiences to grow and rise up past the negative words you may hear. Be the plant that grows! Be the person who helps others grow around you.

Self-Care Round Up

A weekly self check-in can help you maintain focus on your thoughts, feelings, and actions. What did you accomplish last week? What things did you do well? What are you most proud of this week? What challenges did you face? How did you handle them? At the end of each week, check in with yourself. Ask yourself these questions and be sure to praise yourself! You should be proud of doing the hard work of managing your fast, powerful emotions!

As you begin your check-in, please remember:

There is no perfect or right way to manage feelings.

Growing and learning from mistakes is part of the process.

Relying on your supportive people is a strength, not a weakness.

You are the only you, and you are awesome.

You can navigate the tough stuff in life.

"A racing car is an animal with a thousand adjustments."

—MARIO ANDRETTI

All My Emotions

Congratulations on making it to the end of this journal! You now have the training, skills, and experience to drive your super-powerful brain and its many emotions! You are a master of managing your emotions!

Your final task involves creating your own "My Emotions" picture. Use this as a way to summarize and visualize the pieces of this journal that resonated with you.

On a separate piece of paper draw six circles. Make sure the circles are big enough so that you write inside them.

In each of the circles write down one topic on managing emotions that you learned from this journal. Here's a few topics from the book to get you started:

Self Care

Mindfulness

Mantras

Practicing Gratitude

Radical Acceptance

Name It to Tame It

Finding Empathy

S.T.O.P.

Belly Breathing

Now think about each of those themes and comp up with three activities or qualities to support each goal.

Make a small promise to yourself to work on one circle each week. When you've finished, go back through the circles and work on them again and again. Remember to keep at it—learning how to better manage your emotions is an ongoing practice. I know you're going to do great!

Resources

Books

A Teen's Guide to the 5 Love Languages by Gary Chapman and Paige Haley Drygas

An adult or teen coloring book

The Mindfulness Journal for Teens: Prompts and Practices to Help You Stay Cool, Calm, and Present by Jennie Marie Battistin

Apps

Calm Harm: helps teens resist or manage the urge to self-harm

Headspace: for meditation and sleep

Insight Timer: for body scan and mindfulness exercises

MyLife Meditation: for meditation

My3: For teens who struggle with suicidal thoughts. Includes links to three trusted contacts you add to the app, as well as 911 and the National Suicide Hotline. Also includes coping strategies and distractions.

Websites

National Institute of Mental Health: "Shareable Resources on Child and Adolescent Mental Health"

NIMH.NIH.gov/health/education-awareness/shareable-resources-on-child -and-adolescent-mental-health.shtml

Crisis Text Line

CrisisTextLine.org
Text HOME to 741741 to get support 24/7

References

American College of Neuropsychopharmacology. "Lack of sleep could cause mood disorders in teens." December 6, 2017. sciencedaily.com/releases/2017/12/171206090624.htm

Annefrank.org

Cohen-Posey, Kate. Brief Therapy Client Handouts. New York, NY: Wiley, 2000.

Colino, Stacy. "The health Benefits of Expressive Writing," US News, August 31, 2016. Health.usnews.com/wellness/articles/2016-08-31/the-health-benefits-of-expressive-writing

Coyle, Daisy, ADP. "How Being Happy Makes You Healthier." August, 27, 2017. Healthline.com/nutrition/happiness-and-health

Harvard Health. "Giving Thanks Can Make You Happier." Harvard Health. Accessed March 31, 2021. health.harvard.edu/healthbeat/giving-thanks-can-make-you-happier.

Horowitz, J., & Graf, N. Most U.S. teens SEE anxiety, depression as major problems. Retrieved March 31, 2021, from pewresearch.org/social-trends/2019/02/20/most-u-s-teens-see-anxiety-and-depression-as-a-major-problem-among-their-peers/

Krans, Brian, "Nine Ways Stress Is More Dangerous Than You Think." August 4, 2016. Healthline.com/health-news/mental-eight-ways-stress-harms-your-health-082713#1.-Stress-makes-it-difficult-to-control-your-emotions

Larun L, Nordheim LV, Ekeland E, Hagen KB, Heian F. "Exercise in prevention and treatment of anxiety and depression among children and young people." Cochrane Database Syst Rev. 2006 Jul 19;(3):CD004691. doi: 10.1002/14651858.CD004691.pub2. PMID: 16856055.

Majewski, Lori. "9 Empowering Mantras to Shift Your Mindset," Sonima.com. June 7, 2019. sonima.com/meditation/mantras/.

Mayo Clinic. "Depression and anxiety: Exercise eases symptoms." September,27, 2019. Mayoclinic.org/diseases-conditions/depression/in-depth/depression-and-exercise/art-20046495

National Geographic Kids. "Discover the Fascinating World of the Human Brain!" Accessed March 31, 2021. Natgeokids.com/uk/discover/science/general-science/human-brain/

New York University. "Even mild stress can make it difficult to control your emotions." ScienceDaily. Accessed June 19, 2021. sciencedaily.com/releases/2013/08/130826180520.htm.

Parker, Toni, PhD. "6 Steps to Mindfully Deal with Difficult Emotions," The Gottman Institute. September 28, 2016. Gottman.com/blog/6stepstomindfullydealwithdifficultemotions/

Paruthi, S., Brooks, L. J., D'Ambrosio, C., Hall, W. A., Kotagal, S., Lloyd, R. M., Malow, B. A., Maski, K., Nichols, C., Quan, S. F., Rosen, C. L., Troester, M. M., & Wise, M. S. (2016). "Recommended Amount of Sleep for

Pediatric Populations: A Consensus Statement of the American Academy of Sleep Medicine." Journal of clinical sleep medicine : JCSM : official publication of the American Academy of Sleep Medicine, 12(6), 785–786.https://doi.org/10.5664/jcsm.5866

Psychology Today. "Dialectical Behavior Therapy." Accessed March 31, 2021. psychologytoday.com Dialecticalbehaviortherapy.com/distress-tolerance/radical-acceptance/

Psychology Today "Gratitude." Accessed March 31, 2021. https://www.psychologytoday.com/us/basics/gratitude.

Reference.com. "How Many Words Do We Speak in a Day?" Reference. IAC Publishing. Accessed March 31, 2021. reference.com/world-view/many-words-speak-day-68b7ff8bd0b6943e.

Racco, Marilisa, "IKEA conducts bullying experiment on plants — the results are shocking, Global News. May 18, 2018. Globalnews.ca/news/4217594/bully-a-plant-ikea/

Schab, Lisa M. The Anxiety Workbook for Teens: Activities to Help You Deal with Anxiety and Worry. Oakland, CA: New Harbinger Publications, 2008.

Scott, Elizabeth, MS. "Body Scan Meditation. "Very Well Mind. Accessed March 31, 2021. Verywellmind.com/body-scan-meditation-why-and-how-3144782

The Laws of Attraction. "What Is The Law Of Attraction? And How To Use It Effectively." The Law Of Attraction, February 17, 2021. thelawofattraction.com/what-is-the-law-of-attraction/.

Acknowledgments

Thank you to the teens and families I have worked with throughout the years. It was an honor to listen to your stories - the joys and the sorrows. Thank you for trusting me to be a small part of your lives, and for teaching me to laugh, adapt, and be open to learning something new every day.

Thank you also to Callisto Media for the opportunity to share my ideas. All of you have been so supportive and patient as I learned how the world of publishing works.

About the Author

 **Joy A. Hartman, MSW, LCSW,** is a licensed clinical social worker in Wisconsin. She graduated from Carroll University in Waukesha, Wisconsin, and went on to earn a master's in social work at the University of Wisconsin-Milwaukee. She has been working as a family therapist for nearly 30 years. She is the cofounder of a school-based mental health program that brings mental health counseling into area schools. Joy is passionate about empowering teens to become strong, confident adults! She believes every teen has unique strengths and uses those to help them build resiliency. As the parent of three teenagers of her own, Joy has a unique perspective of both professional and personal experiences that guide her in supporting teens and parents as they navigate challenges and mental health concerns.

Follow Joy on her blog at JoyHartman.com or on Facebook.

CPSIA information can be obtained
at www.ICGtesting.com
Printed in the USA
JSHW012035180721
16984JS00002B/7

9 781638 073390